Sun

Wind

Cast

Boy

Girl

Speaker

1

Speaker: Once upon a time, Wind and Sun had an argument about who was stronger.

 **Wind** Sun, I am stronger than you. I am the strongest thing in the world.

Speaker: Wind let out a big puff. The trees shook. Big waves rose up in the sea.

Speaker: Sun looked at Wind. Sun had a sweet smile and a soft voice.

 **Sun** You may be louder than I am but you are not stronger than I am!

 **Wind** Yes, I am! I am the strongest, grandest, biggest thing in the world. When I blow clouds, the sky gets darker. When I blow waves, the quiet sea gets wilder.

Wind All you do is sit and shine all day long.

Sun When I shine, the world gets nice and warm. Let's have a contest. We'll see who is the strongest.

 **Wind** That's a fine plan. What shall we do?

 **Sun** See that girl with the cape and that boy with the hat?

 **Wind** I see them. So what's the contest?

Sun  We shall see who can get the girl to take off her cape and the boy to take off his hat. Whoever does that first wins the contest.

Wind Fine! I'll win in no time. What prize will I get?

9

Sun You will get the finest present you can imagine. On the biggest banner you have ever seen, it will say "Strongest in the World." To get it, you must win the contest first.

the World

Wind I can't wait! Let's start the contest right away. I'll get that cape and hat off in no time! Let me go first.

Speaker: So Wind started to blow. All her thoughts were on winning. She blew harder and harder. Clouds raced through the sky. Branches broke off trees.

Speaker: The girl hugged her cape closer to her. The boy held on tighter to his hat, pulling it down over his eyes. The wind blew harder and harder but the children just pulled their things tighter and tighter.

Speaker: At last, Wind was not able to blow one more puff. She was worn out. Then it was Sun's turn. As she shined, the day got warmer and warmer.

Speaker: It was getting hotter and hotter and hotter. First, the girl took off her cape. Then the boy took off his hat. What a fine day it was!

 **Sun** Now tell me, Wind, who is stronger — you or I?

Speaker: What could Wind say? She had huffed and puffed, but Sun was the winner.

So here's the lesson of this play: **You can be nice and still be strong.**